DIVINE WHISPERS

365 SPIRITUAL QUOTES OF H.H. SRI SRI RAVI SHANKAR

RAVI VALLURI

Leadstart
INKSTATE

ISBN: 978-93-90040-57-5

First published in India 2021 by Leadstart Inkstate
A Division of One Point Six Technologies Pvt Ltd

Sales Office:
Unit No.25/26, Building No.A/1,
Near Wadala RTO,
Wadala (East), Mumbai – 400037 India
Phone: +91 969933000
Email: info@leadstartcorp.com
www.leadstartcorp.com

Disclaimer: The views expressed in this book are those of the Author and do not pertain to be held by the Publisher.

Editor: Cora Bhatia
Cover: Ashwini Jadhav
Layouts: Ashwini Jadhav

DEDICATED TO

Vasudaiva Kutambakam

(One World Family)

BOOKS BY THE SAME AUTHOR

The Matter of the Mind

Manomoolamidham (Telugu translation of The Matter of the Mind, translated by Dr Y. Shiva Ram Prashad)

Make the Mind Mt.Kailasa

The Infinite Mind (co-authored with Ankush Garg)

NaMo 303 Words to Victory.

Indian Stories: Images & Thoughts

HEARTBREAK AT COFFEE SHOP An Array of Tales

ABOUT THE AUTHOR

Ravi Valluri is an officer of the Indian Railway Traffic Service and has worked at several places on different zonal railways.

He has also served in Mil Rail (Army Headquarters), where he was decorated with the Chief of Army Staff award. Currently, he is posted at Prayagraj (Uttar Pradesh, India) as the Principal Chief Operations Manager, North Central Railway.

The author is also a faculty of the Art of Living Foundation. He conducts the Happiness Programme, yoga and meditation sessions of the foundation, besides helping counsel addicts and undertaking courses for those dependent on alcohol and drugs.

He has had a penchant for theatre, public speaking and writing since his school days and continues to fuel these interests.

He is a regular blogger at Word Press and Speaking Tree besides writing for the Free Press Journal, Mumbai.

He can be reached at valluri.ravi@gmail.com

ACKNOWLEDGEMENTS

On December 9, 2006, I stopped drinking. I have now had more than a decade of sobriety.

Gradually, I am trying to mend relationships with my family, friends, and the world. It is indeed providential and divine benediction that the very people I hurt stood by me, while I confronted innumerable misadventures and unwelcome situations in my roller-coaster life. Indisputably, it is a testimony to the mental robustness and faith of my parents, my late maternal grandmother and, in particular, my wife, who accepted me despite all my predilections.

'Accept people and situations as they are' is a sutra of the Art of Living Foundation.

They perfected the craft as I undertook the courses offered by the Foundation. Their faith in the mystical Vishistadvaita saint Shri Raghavendra Swami of Mantralayam and chanting of three holy books–Hanuman Chalisa, Sundara Kanda and Vayu Stuti provided them succour.

I am profoundly grateful to H. H. Sri Sri Ravi Shankar, without whose grace and blessings I would not have traversed this path and eschewed the dependency on alcohol and tobacco. My deep gratitude to the Art of Living Foundation for the various programmes it offers and to its extended family, which has provided me with innumerable opportunities to interact with a cross-section of people and helped me to develop into a brawny individual.

There are thousands of teachers in the Art of Living. However, singular in their positive approach and those who shaped my thoughts are Shri Kishore Mukherjee, Shri Arun Madhavan, Commodore Rao and Shri Vinod Menon. It will be a travesty on my part if I do not acknowledge their contribution in fashioning my personality.

In 2015, H. H. Sri Sri Ravi Shankar at the Gandipet ashram, Hyderabad, said in his inimitable manner, "You start writing and soon your works will be published." Thus, my maiden effort, 'The Matter of the Mind' was created. Gurudev unveiled the book on Vijayadasami in 2016, and I am eternally grateful to him. The journey in writing and the forays have helped me to grow as an individual. Through the Divine grace of the Master, I have written six books.

My son, Siddhartha and daughter, Tejala have always been critical in appraising the quality and content of my work. It is through the prism of their minds that I am able to view the thought processes of the current generation. My wife Lakshmi Valluri has helped me, as in my other ventures, to embellish this work and in particular selection of the quotations.

I am grateful to Pooja Dutt of Leadstart Publishing who had first evaluated the manuscript, also to Trupti Sawardekar, the project head and my editor Cora Bhatia.

CONTENTS

GOD/ALMIGHTY

"When you know you own God, you will not be in a hurry to get something out of God."

"When you have infinite patience, you will realise God belongs to you."

"God does not test you because he knows you completely –your past, present and future."

"God is calling you every moment."

"God is the Seer himself who sees—that is God."

"God is love. Being in love is sharing that love."

"This entire universe is made up of God. There is nothing outside God."

"God is responsibility, total responsibility."

"If you pray to God with all your heart, (dropping the sorrow which simply means hanging onto the past) then whatever you desire will be given to you."

"God exists in everyone but they are asleep in some people that is why they exhibit demonic qualities."

"Just like how all raindrops will reach the ocean, same way all prayers will reach the same God."

"God is attribute-less but all attributes belong to him as nothing exists beyond God."

"Love shakes everything. Even the angels and God. That is what happens after Sata Chandi Homa, you dance."

"Nature loves to give you surprises. God loves fun. He always gives you surprises – sometimes pleasant, sometimes unpleasant."

"God is that space in which everything is, was and will be."

"God is beyond the three qualities: *Sattva, Rajas and Tamas.* Yet the qualities exist in him!"

"Don't run after anybody. You are important in your life. Focus on your career, acquiring talents and doing *seva* for society. If at all you have to please anybody, please God, please the Divine and please yourself."

"Listening to God is meditation. Asking God is prayer."

"The experience in you is God."

"Parashuram avatars teach you to see God even in the cruel
person!"

"God is asleep in every particle of this universe. God is in you in seed form. When he wakes up, neither you nor the world remain."

GURU

"The Master is a doorway."

"The Master is presence. The world is relativity and relativity has limitations. Presence is unlimited."

"If you are not feeling close to the Master, it is because of you,
because of your mind, because of your ego concepts."

"A Master is like an ocean. Ocean is there, readily available. It does
not reject anybody."

"If a Master is not hollow and empty; he is no Master at all."

"Guru Purnima is the day of reflection. It is the New Year for a spiritual seeker; for one who is on the path. Just like you have the calendar New Year on 1st January every year, for a spiritual seeker, the New Year is on Guru Purnima."

"Like there is fatherhood and motherhood, there is something called Guruhood as well, and you all have to play the role of Guruhood to someone or the other. Anyways, consciously or unconsciously, you are all a Guru to somebody already because you do give advice, guidance, love and care to people, isn't it? So now do it consciously, giving your hundred per cent without expecting anything in return. *This is living the Guru Principle.*"

"Know that there is no difference between you, the Divine and the Guru Principle. It all culminates into just one thing – the queen bee. And meditation is reposing in the atman."

"On GuruPurnima, ask for what you want and it will be bestowed. Go for the highest desire. *The best wish is to desire for knowledge and freedom.* Think about everything in your life that you can be grateful for, and ask what you want for the future. And bless others; this is the time to bless people. Just receiving is not enough; we need to also bless those who are in need."

"So feel grateful for all the blessings that you have received. Be grateful for all the knowledge, and see how knowledge has transformed life. *Without the knowledge we will be nowhere* – realizing this, feel grateful for all that has come our way, and celebrate! Thank all the Masters of the tradition who have preserved this knowledge from ages, and brought it to us. It is very significant."

"Lord Krishna said, '*Mam ekamsharanamvraja*', meaning, '*Come to me alone*'
He said this to his dearest disciple Arjuna to make his mind *totally be there* to value the present."

"When you have a Guru; fear, uncertainty, these things simply don't come."

"The Guru is not the (physical) body. The Guru is the Divine light that resides within the body; the Guru is love."

"Just to toss a ball from one end to another, or to learn how to hit a puck with a stick, we need a coach or a guide. Then how can one not need a guide for spirituality? A Guru is definitely needed."

"You should never say this; God has become a problem for you. If you long for God, or for your Guru, in your heart, then that is good. This takes you on the path of progress. If that longing is not there then there is no juice in life."

"Guru and Shishya*parampara* is always one on one, but in the crowd!"

"Know that it's all one – Shiva Tattva, Guru Tattva, AtmaTattva. The differences are only in the name (flavours)."

"Guru doesn't look for intelligence in a disciple. He creates an opportunity where, the intelligence that is already there blossoms."

"Why or how is it that only a Guru can bring about a change in a person? It is because a Guru never wants anything for himself. A Guru wants transformation in someone only because what the person is doing is harming himself or herself. A Guru looks at people with this compassionate perspective which is why people transform when they come to Him."

"The Guru is the one who leads you to the light of the Divine (Govind). So it is right. The Guru has always held the highest position in our country since the ages. It is a very unique pedestal and we need to preserve and honour the dignity of the Guru."

"A Guru always wants his disciples to make great progress so that they may surpass and defeat the Guru himself one day. Then a Guru's job is done."

KNOWLEDGE

"Be a friend in knowledge. Uplift each other in knowledge."

"Knowledge is a burden if it does not set you free."

"Knowledge keeps everything fresh."

"In science you have knowledge first, and then faith follows. In spirituality, faith comes first, and then knowledge follows."

"When you follow fun, misery follows you. When you follow knowledge, fun follows you."

"Illusion is error of perception and knowing illusion as illusion is knowledge."

"Suffering is a product of limited knowledge."

"For one who has awakened in knowledge, there is no more suffering."

"If too many desires come in your mind, or too much restlessness and agitation then food, atmosphere and association have been the cause."

"Wise is the one who learns from another's mistakes. Less wise is the one who learns only from his own mistakes. The fool keeps making the same mistakes again and again and never learns from them. Knowledge is a burden if it robs you of innocence."

"Another wealth is having different skills and talents. Some people write well, some are good in arguing, some are good in debating, some have a knack for music, some have a wonderful voice, some cook well, some are talented in bringing up a child, some are good in administration, and so on. There are people who put their maximum efforts to achieve what they want. Yet, they fail to achieve their goal. So effort alone is not enough to achieve one's goal, you need the wealth of skill."

"The world is full of lessons if only we observe it with full awareness. Be as humble as the grass, then nothing can touch you, nothing. No one can humiliate you. In the eyes of the divine, it is those who serve the creation that are the true kings and queens. Walk like a king and be a perfect servant!"

"Our memory is very short. It appears this is the only life. We are not aware of our Source. The moment you become aware of your source and your infinite past, your whole life changes – like somebody suddenly becoming aware of how wealthy he (or she) is. It causes a shift in the awareness. Suddenly, you become aware, Oh! I have several billions of dollars in my bank account! Your style of walking will change immediately! This is the awareness of the Source. You don't even have to remember all the drama that you went through. It's enough if you just remember the source. The memory of the source is a great wealth. It makes life one continuous stream – not 'cut off' – not in pieces."

KARMA

"When you praise someone, you take on their good karma. When you blame someone, you take on their bad karma."

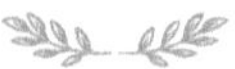

"Prarabdha karma cannot be changed. Sanchita karma can be changed by spiritual practices."

"Despite being amidst all pleasures and worldly things, one is completely untouched, untainted and unstained by the events and happenings."

"Look at the events come, pass and go. According to their own law of karma, both pleasant and unpleasant events come and pass through you."

"Saying anything good happens through grace and anything bad happens through karma, keeps you grounded."

"You deal with the situation. All that you face in life are result of your karma. It could be latent or present karma."

"Every bad karma has a remedy – compassion, meditation, chanting and charity."

"You can rise above the ocean of karma through awareness."

"When you increase your sense of knowingness, your karma gets reduced. For example, you feel like throttling somebody, but because you are aware, you don't do it."

"A Yogi works hundred per cent, without desires or attachments. This is Karma Yoga."

"There are certain karmas which can't be changed but many of them can be."

"Until the impression of your previously done karma is on your mind, that karma manages to exist. You are freed from karma once the impression is erased."

"Dedicated action, focused action is Karma Yoga. Through Karma Yoga also one can attain me (Krishna)."

"It's your desire or attachment that causes tiredness, not the work. Karma Yoga is acting hundred per cent, even though you aren't attached."

"Once you get human body, karma begins because intellect has choice."

"Many things like food, time, company, planetary positions, place and our karmas can affect the quality of your *sadhana*."

"Every impression is karma, but there is nothing to worry about because karma is not like an engraving on a rock – it is fluid. And karma is always bound by time because every action has only a limited reaction – it is not infinite."

"Reaction and non-action both create karma, but conscious action transcends karma."

DEATH

"Death dwells in the void as well as in celebration."

"Death brings you in touch with the reality of life."

"Wake up and see your life is too short. The realization that life is short will bring dynamism to your life."

"Life works on strange laws of nature (Karma).
One never knows when a friend turns enemy and vice-versa.
Rely on your Self; self-reliance."

"This temporary world is of death. Here, everything dies and everything changes. Do you recognise that subtle field of energy, that subatomic level of energy that does not change? Objects disintegrate, but atoms remain the same. Atoms and molecules disintegrate, but the sub-atomic particles are the same. All these human bodies are different, but there is one field of energy, the mind, that flows through everybody. Do you realize that there is one thing –your true nature?"

"You are free the moment you see it's not in you. If you have a pain, observe it's happening in the body. If there is tightness or joy in your mind, observe that it is tight, sad, unhappy or happy. Just observe that you are not enjoying, and it is happening elsewhere, as though it is happening, knows that there is no death to the disciple. *Atma* never dies. Even after death he continues to get direction on the path."

"Will we remember anything from this life after we die?"

"Knowledge of life brings confidence. Knowledge of death makes
you fearless."

"What is death? And what is beyond death? Nature has provided a tiny glimpse of death to you in everyday life- your sleep. It's akin to your sleep. When you are awake, you are engaged in all various activities, and the moment you hit the bed, what happens to you, where do you go? However, the day has been, pleasant or unpleasant; sleep provides you the deep rest."

"Life is much larger than birth and death, failure and success. You are the unblemished, pure eternal Self. Knowing this you will walk like a King."

"Those who meditate do not fear death. The one, who is filled with fears, faces death at every step, but for the one steeped in Divine Love, there is no death!"

"The spirit or the energy has no birth and no death. There is something deep inside of you that was never born and that never will die."

"Everything you do, do it happily, with contentment; that brings you liberation from the cycle of birth and death."

"You know, at the time of death, only two questions will be before us: How much love have we shared, and how much knowledge have we gained in our lifetime."

"All places of worship in all religions are connected with places of
burial or cremation because only the awareness of death can bring
dispassion and can ground you in knowledge."

YOGA

"Yoga is something that makes you happy, something that uplifts your spirit, something which makes you strong, vibrant, and powerful, why would you not do it?"

"Like a flower bud, human life has the potential to blossom fully. Blossoming of human potential to fullness is yoga."

"Yoga brings the knowledge, passion and action together."

"Yoga is a study of life, study of your body, breath, mind, intellect, memory, and ego; study of your inner faculties."

"Withdraw your senses from the object to its source, then the union happens, then yoga happens."

"Peace is our very nature, and yoga leads you to inner peace."

"The purpose of yoga is to stop suffering even before it arises."

"Yoga is not just a weight-loss program; it is a science to make you feel lighter. You lose mental stuff of anger, jealousy, hatred, greed, etc."

"One of the rules of yoga is to cultivate the practice of being happy."

"The wisdom of yoga transforms one from arrogance to self-confidence, meekness to humility, from dependence to a realization of interdependence."

"The wisdom of yoga transforms one from craving for freedom to recognition of unboundedness, from limited ownership to oneness with the whole."

"Peace is our very nature, and yoga leads you to inner peace. Yoga is a study of life, study of your body, breath, mind, intellect, memory, and ego. Study of your inner faculties! We do yoga to make life more beautiful, to stop misery from entering our world."

"Yoga is the best app that everyone must download in their life."

"A disease-free body, a violence-free society, a confusion-free mind, an inhibition-free intellect, a trauma-free memory, a sorrow-free soul and a quiver-free breath is the impact that yoga can make on your life."

"If you claim that you are a Yogi, then you should have an undying smile on your face. I would say, that is the sign of a Yogi. Yoga makes your emotions softer and more peaceful, and you blossom in your emotions. It brings freedom in your expression and your thought patterns."

"Many people think of the eight limbs of Yoga as a step-wise process to go level by level. They think that one has to strive to become proficient in one level before ascending to the next. This is not really so. I would say that all these eight limbs or aspects of yoga are woven together and happen simultaneously."

"When a child is conceived in the womb, then all its organs are formed together. It is not that first, the feet are formed and then the arms take shape. No, it is not so. All the limbs and organs develop together. This is why we must take all these eight aspects or limbs of Yoga together at every step. Only then can we experience the fullness and totality of yoga, and can bring about an extraordinary transformation and experience in our life."

"Yoga is not just only postures; it is your state of being."

"Yoga is vast and has many possibilities. This message we must bring to the people. The spiritual aspect of yoga should be highlighted. That alone can bring up the happiness factor in society."

LOVE

"Usually, when people love something and there is a longing for it, they try to get rid of it because it is painful. The more you try to run away from it; you are destroying not only the longing but also the love."

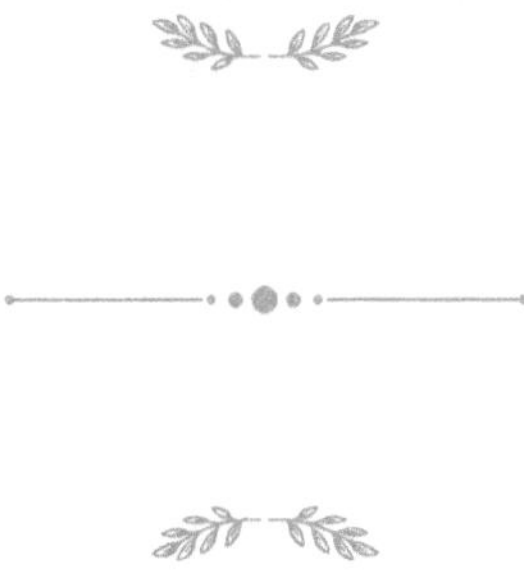

"Love is incomplete and it will have to remain incomplete. It means that you have marked the boundaries, found its limitations. For love to be infinite, it has to be incomplete. Love is infinite and it finds expression in infinite ways."

"A devotee is like a crazy person in the eyes of ignorant people.
They are not bothered about what people think or say about them.
A devotee's world is nothing but God."

"There are three kinds of love. The love that comes out of charm,
that which comes out of comfort, and the divine love."

"Seeing the Divine in your valentine and make the Divinity your Valentine (your sweet beloved). Just Be and know that you are Loved, that is beloved."

"There is strength in peace. There is strength in calmness. There is strength in love, but it goes unnoticed. What you cannot win with guns, you can win through love, and this power of love needs to be realised."

"The most powerful thing in the world is love! We can win the hearts of people through love."

"You cannot transform the world when a terrorist is at your door, but is there some way in which can transform the world? Is there any alternative method that can bring sense to people who do not listen to anything, other than force? We can start thinking along these lines only when we realise that there is enormous power in love and inner peace."

"We can all radiate peace, good thoughts, good vibrations; good wishes and that will definitely make an impact on the planet."

"We need to get back pride in being non-violent."

"Love is not an emotion; it is your very existence."

"Here are the signs of love. When you love someone, you see nothing wrong with them."

"When you love someone, you want to see them always happy and
you want them to have the best."

"Love is the highest strength, yet it makes you absolutely weak."

"Love cannot tolerate distance, and hatred cannot tolerate nearness."

"You can experience love, but you cannot describe it or express it totally."

"Love is beyond sight, touch, smell, taste, and sound."

"When there is love, there is no ego. Ego dissolves like the dew drops with the sun."

"In the company of one who is living love, you also can't but spring into that love."

"Love is that phenomenon of dissolving, disappearing, merging, becoming one with the Infinite."

"Love is that phenomenon of total letting go."

"The seers, the scene, and the process of seeing all merge. The knowledge, the knower, and the known, they all merge, become one and that is divine love."

"The path of love is not a tedious path. It's a path of joy. It's a path of singing and dancing."

"Respect for the Self is faith and faith is being open."

"Have respect for the Self and no one can take your self-respect."

"Someone does not need to be great in order to be respected. Respecting life makes you great."

LOYALTY

"Loyalty is commitment to a cause or a person, irrespective of the situation and changes that time brings upon. Loyalty transcends promises and performances."

"It is unjust to demand loyalty from everybody, with the exception being party workers and office bearers who have to be loyal to their party as otherwise it will not function."

"Democracy and loyalty are two diametrically opposite concepts;
yet they are compatible when they are in their rightful places."

"In the US, a common expression is 'yellow-dog Democrats' –
people loyal to the Democrats would rather vote for a yellow dog
than a Republican. Most people label themselves as Republicans
or Democrats. In any election, it's the narrow swing vote, which is
really the deciding factor. If you watch closely, it is only a few who
have really chosen. Ideally, it should be the masses that choose and
the few who should be loyal. Then election has meaning."

"You can do better than a formal post, as did Mahatma Gandhi."

"It is the nature of people with integrity to find an anchor for their loyalty."

"Life needs loyalty, but when it comes to democracy, one should act like a father who has love for all his sons, yet chooses the right one for the right job. Youhave to be loyal to human values. Instead, if you are loyal to a party how can you exercise your franchise? You cannot be loyal to a party and claim to have a choice. Only the impartial can choose."

"Loyalty disallows impartial competition for if you are loyal to one political party and if the same party continues to rule, what is the point in having elections?"

"Loyalty has its place. You need to be loyal to your principles, monarch, country, the military, your employer, employees and spouse. You have to be faithful to your country, but you endanger democracy if you are loyal to a single political party."

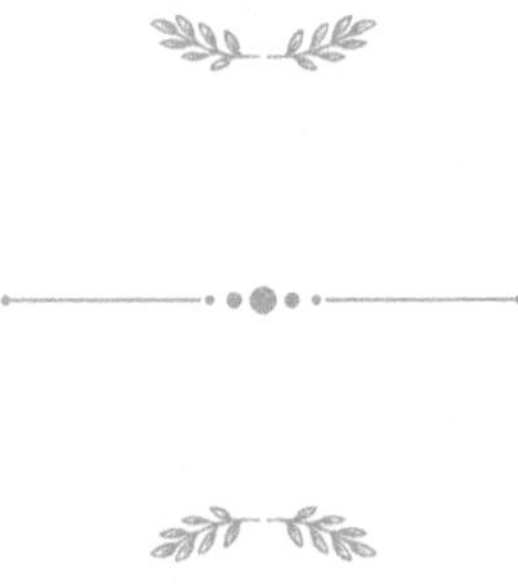

"Loyalty is the way in which a mature and integrated mind behaves. Loyalty indicates undivided wholeness of consciousness and shows richness of the mind. When the mind is not integrated, it is feverish, disloyal and opportunistic."

"A divided mind will gradually lead to schizophrenia and other physical and mental disorders. Loyalty is a real strength and will have the support of nature in the long run."

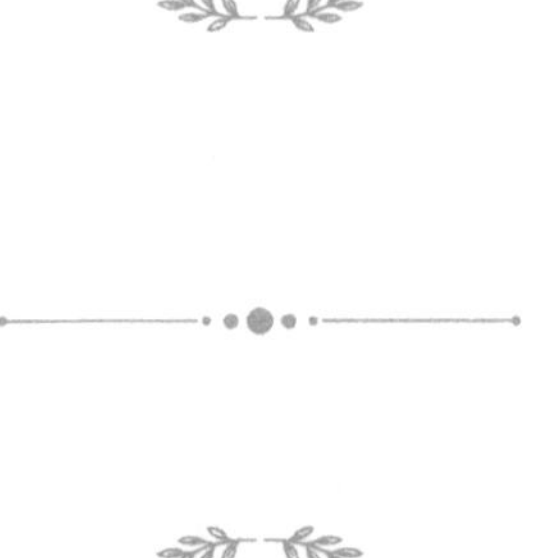

"Fear and ambitions are impediments to loyalty. Loyalty is needed in both the material and spiritual plane. Either to destroy, create or maintain any institution, group or society, loyalty is essential."

"Freedom and loyalty should go hand in hand. However, loyalty which is stifling gradually decays and freedom without loyalty leads to anarchy."

"A loyal mind is a 'yes-mind'. The purpose of asking questions is to get an answer. The purpose of all answers is to create a 'yes'. 'Yes' is an acknowledgement of knowledge. The 'yes-mind' is a quiet, holistic and joyful mind. The 'no-mind' is an agitated, doubting and miserable mind."

"Loyalty begins with a 'yes-mind' and starts to perish with a 'no-mind'."

"Disloyalty comes out of opportunism. Opportunism is short sightedness of one's destiny. Integrity or wholeness is essential to be healthy."

"Loyalty means believing in the continuity of commitment, honouring commitment. It takes you beyond the duality of craving and aversion. Responsibility, dedication and commitment are the limbs of loyalty."

ANGER

"In ignorance anger is cheap and a smile is costly."

"Make your smile cheaper and your anger expensive."

"The anger of the enlightened is a blessing."

"Why can't we control our anger? Because we love perfection.
Make a little room for imperfection in our lives."

"Anger is a distortion of your true nature and it doesn't allow the self to shine forth fully. Showing anger itself is not wrong, but being unaware of your anger only hurts you."

"You may remind yourself a hundred times that you shouldn't get angry, but when the emotion comes, you are unable to control it. It comes like a thunderstorm."

"All anger is about something which has already happened. Is it of any use getting angry about something that you cannot alter? The mind always vacillates between the past and the future. When the mind is in the past, it's angry about something that has already happened, but anger is meaningless as we can't alter the past. And when the mind is in the future, it's anxious about something that may or may not happen. When the mind is in the present moment, anxiousness and anger appear so meaningless."

"Meditation is letting go of anger from the past and the events of the past. Meditation is accepting this moment and living every moment totally with depth. Often anger comes because you do not accept the present moment."

"Anger comes when one seeks too much of perfection. When you are joyful, you don't look for perfection. If you are always looking for perfection then you are not at the source of joy."

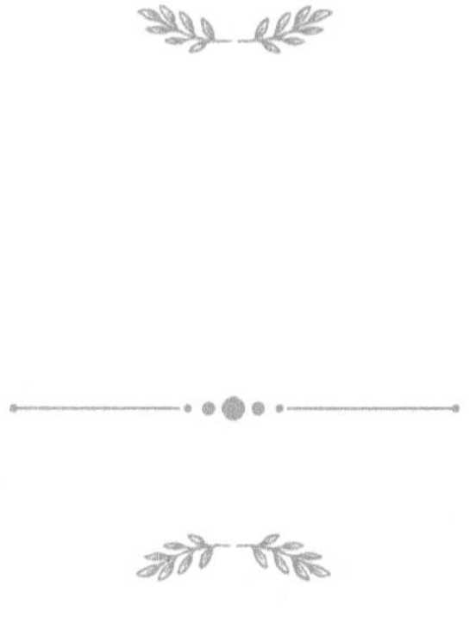

"Religion keeps society divided. Spirituality unites it."

"Anger is not bad if it is under your control, and if you sparingly use it, it works."

SEVA/SERVICE

"If you are not having good experiences in meditation, then do more seva you will gain merit and your meditation will be deeper. When you bring some relief or freedom to someone through seva, good vibrations and blessings come to you.
Seva brings merit; merit allows you to go deep in meditation; meditation brings back your smile."

"When you make service the sole purpose in life, it eliminates fear, focuses your mind, and gives you meaning."

"Be grateful for any opportunity to do seva."

"When celebration becomes service, there is no guilt. And when service becomes celebration, there is no pride."

"Identify with the virtues and know that negativity is just a visitor. In time, the virtues manifest with help of meditation and service."

"Through meditation find happiness within. Through service spread happiness outside."

"Guru never asks you to stay in Ashram. He asks you to be happy and do *seva* (service)."

"When someone does service in their life, they experience contentment, satisfaction."

"Often one looks for contentment through pleasure. True contentment can only come through service."

"The willingness and ability to do service comes only when you don't have any botheration. So come to the Guru and drop all your botheration, and joyfully do service."

"Spirituality is nothing but caring and sharing; offering oneself in service."

"It is time for us to encourage our children to learn music and spend time in doing service to the society, and to develop a scientific temper while also pursuing spiritual and dharmic knowledge."

"Politics is not a place to earn money but to do service."

"What is needed to blossom fully is a combination of sensitivity and sensibility."

"Just do service. Don't think too much, whether it's selfless/selfish. Never mind. Don't analyse too much. Let's keep it simple."

LIFE

"Have you ever thought what the purpose of your life is? What is life all about? Such questions are very precious. When they dawn in your mind, only then does your life begin."

"To know what you are on this planet for; ask yourself what you are not here for!"

"Life involves ups and downs which is very natural. Do not be afraid
of this. Every pinch that you have in life is for the best."

"In Buddha's life you don't see any imperfection. Buddha lived a
pure life not for his own sake, but for the sake of the world, for the
sake of the devotees."

"Seeing the whole thing as a drama, that is the only way you can remain in your centre."

"Life has four characteristics, it exists, evolves, expresses and extinguishes. For this, it depends on five elements: the earth, water, air, ether and fire."

"Health is...Disease-free body/ Quiver-free breath/ Stress-free mind/ Inhibition-free intellect/ Obsession-free memory/Ego that includes all. And soul which is free from sorrow."

"Human evolution has two steps –from being somebody to being nobody, and from being nobody to being everybody.
This knowledge can bring sharing and caring throughout the world."

"Life is nothing to be very serious about. Life is a ball in your hands to play with. Don't hold on to the ball."

"Certain amount of certainty in life gives security. But if everything is certain then it becomes dull and boring."

BREATH

"Ninety per cent of the impurities in the body go out through the breath because we are breathing twenty four hours a day. However, we are using only thirty per cent of our lung capacity. We are not breathing enough."

"Learning something about our breath is very important. Our breath has a great lesson to teach us, which we have forgotten, for every rhythm in the mind, there is a corresponding rhythm in the breath, for every rhythm in the breath there is a corresponding emotion. So when you cannot handle your mind directly, through breath you can handle the mind."

"The breath is the link between the body and the mind. If the mind is a kite, the breath is the thread. The longer the thread the higher the kite can go."

"Meditation and breathing techniques help us to get out of the vicious circle of negativity."

"When you get angry, just observe that sensation. Take a few long deep breaths and see if it changes."

"Life is an act of letting go. You breathe in; breathe out. You can't hold on to anything."

"Breath is the link between your body, your spirit and your mind.

"On full moon day, when you look at the moon your breath becomes musical. Looking at the moon, the *prana* in you becomes musical and life becomes harmonious."

"When there is fear, observe the sensations happening inside you.
See what is happening when you are afraid."

"Do some pranayama (breathing exercise). That will help."

"Learn to make people your own. They already belong to you. They come from the same soil and breathe the same air that you expel. You are all connected."

"There is a lot to learn if you watch your breath, and see what is happening. I would like to share about some breathing techniques with you. One of them is about our two nostrils. Have you ever wondered why we have two nostrils? We could have had one big hole! There is a reason. When you breathe through your left nostril, it affects the side of your right brain, and when you breathe through the right nostril, it affects the left side of the brain."

"Scientists have recently found that when you breathe through the right nostril, the metabolism in your body is twice as much as when you breathe through the left nostril."

"Did you know the first thing that we did when we came to this planet was? We took a deep breath in and then we started crying, right?"

"And the last thing that we will do in this life is, breathe out and then make others cry. In birth, you cried and made everybody laugh, and in death, you take the last breath out and make everyone cry. If you don't do that, you have not lived a good life!"

"Breath – It is the most important source of energy. The breath can help us energize our whole system. If you are tired, and you try some breathing exercises, change your breathing pattern, you will feel energetic."

"Millions have come out of trauma and depression through breathing techniques and meditation."

"Meditation and breathing are now being advocated as an alternative to anti-depressants by many medical institutions. So, it just works!"

"Well, I am not an anthropologist, but the connection between the breath and the mind is as old as the connection between the breath and the body. It is from the very beginning."

"In Zen meditation, and also in the tradition of Shintoism here, the movement and chanting is all connected with the breath. When you have the long drawn chanting, you take a deep breath in and then you chant for a long time."

"The connection is there in all the ancient traditions of the world. If you see the Maoris in New Zealand, they greet by exchanging the breath; they rub each other's nose, breathe in and breathe out. This is how they connect, and create harmony between people."

"Lord Buddha also said to just observe your breath, *anapanasati*; he said with this you can observe the sensation, and go beyond to see what your true nature is. The breath has no nationality or religion; it is needed for all mankind."

COMPASSION

"There are two types of compassion. One is the compassion of the wise; one is that of the ignorant."

"Why do you worry? One day everyone is going to go under the ground. You shouldn't wait for that day to be peaceful. Some people say, 'May your soul rest in peace'. We should be in peace vertically not horizontally!"

"Lives will take a new direction if we take pride in non-violence, compassion and service."

"Compassion towards animals is very sacred job. It gives you a sense of inner fulfilment."

"Compassion comes with connectivity and connectivity can happen when you are free from within."

"Passion, dispassion and compassion, know that all three are present in everyone."

CONSCIOUSNESS

Consciousness moving on the surface of the body is stimuli, which causes pleasure. When consciousness shrinks, then the sensation of pain and suffering arises."

"When consciousness moves through the body in limited channels, pleasure is experienced. Repeated enjoyment of the stimuli causes inertia and dullness."

"Fish never closes its eyes, it symbolises being witness consciousness all time. Hence, Vishnu too the first avatar was a fish."

"Often cooks don't enjoy their own food. Listening to the same piece of music loses the charm; people in the sex industry don't enjoy sex. If the stimuli are observed, then consciousness expands and becomes peace."

"Pain is nothing but consciousness wanting to expand and to become free. Freedom basically is liberation from the craving of the stimuli."

CONTENTMENT

"Contentment and Happiness! Do everything happily. Walk, talk, sit happily; even if you complain against somebody, do it happily."

"You can turn every situation into your advantage. Have you ever thought of this? Once you are blossomed from within, you can take any insult and turn it into an advantage."

"Pleasure simply brings more craving. But often one looks for contentment through pleasure. True contentment can only come through service."

"Want, or desire, arises when you are not happy. Have you seen this? When you are very happy then there is this contentment. Contentment means no want."

RESPONSIBILITY

"Only those who can totally detach can take total responsibility. Eventually, you will be able to be both attached and detached simultaneously."

"As a human being, we have responsibilities and needs. If responsibilities are less and needs are more, then we will remain sad and grumbling. If we take up more responsibilities and don't need much for ourselves, then we are happy and more powerful."

"It's the time when our needs are more and we take less responsibility that we are miserable. And when our responsibility is more and our needs are also more, these are times we struggle. And when our responsibility is more and needs are less, we are happy."

ORGANIZATION

"The entire creation is a huge organization. Everything is made up of atoms. The whole world is nothing but organization, where the atoms have decided to organize themselves in a specific pattern to form a particular substance."

"Organization is control. Devotion is chaos!"

“Organization needs attention to details, a material awareness. Organization is being worldly. Devotion is getting lost, forgetting the world, being in ecstasy.”

“Often you lose devotion in organizing. And often in the name of devotion you create chaos and disregard the organization. You have to be a saint to be in both organization and devotion. If you have both, you are on the mark.”

SUDARSHAN KRIYA
The Unique Rhythmic Breathing Technique

"Our breath has a great lesson to teach us, which we have forgotten, for every rhythm in the mind, there is a corresponding rhythm in the breath."

"Every child has creativity in them and this finds an expression when they do meditation, yoga and Sudarshan Kriya."

"You know what the first act was when you came into this world?
It was taking a breath in. And your last act will be breathing out."

"*Prana* means subtle life force energy. *Aayama* means directing or controlling. So, Pranayama means directing the life force energy. Pranayama is housing our awareness."

"*Su* means proper, *Darshan* means vision and *Kriya* is a purifying action. Through the action of our breath, we get a proper vision of who we really are."

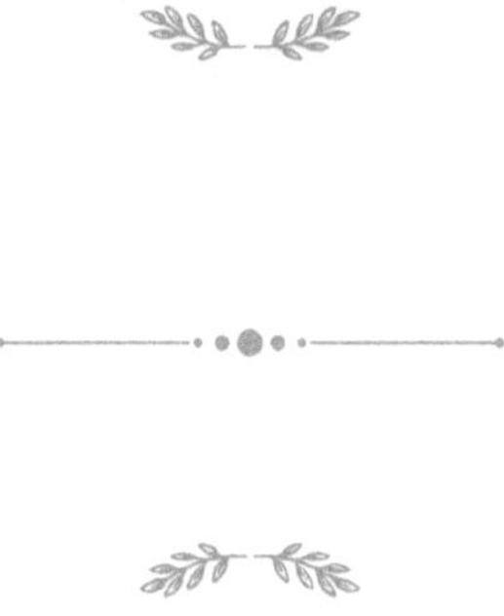

"In Sudarshan Kriya we will be experiencing the rhythm of being. We will be using rhythms of the breath to harmonise the different levels of our Self. It is like the difference between noise and music."

"When sounds are harmonised to a rhythm, we call it music. Enlightenment is not gaining anything but harmonising our whole system rhythmically."

"Sudarshan Kriya leads you to that inner space – a state of thoughtlessness, a state of stillness and the art of meditation helps you go deep into that state. So, they complement each other. If you meditate after the Sudarshan Kriya, your meditation is deeper. And if you are meditating regularly, the Kriya becomes easier and more natural."

"You can't say that the body leads the mind or the mind leads the body. What you can say is that the body, breath and mind getting into the rhythm is Sudarshan Kriya. Finding that inner harmony and depth, and manifesting it on the surface, on the physical level of the body and breath is meditation. Through mantra, you go to the deepest level of your consciousness and bring that to expression in your day-to-day activity. That is meditation."

"Through meditation and Sudarshan Kriya, you will see how the grief gets vaporized."

"Domestic and social violence arise out of stress. We never teach people how to handle stress. No one is given spiritual knowledge. Don't you think this knowledge of meditation and Sudarshan Kriya should reach everybody? This knowledge of non-violence should reach all."

"Nature is replete with various rhythms and cycles – day follows night, night follows day, seasons come and go. Similarly, there are biological rhythms to our bodies, minds and emotions. When these rhythms are in sync, we feel a sense of harmony and well-being."

"The Sudarshan Kriya incorporates specific natural rhythms of breath which harmonize the rhythms of the body and emotions and bring them in tune with the rhythms of nature. The breath connects the body and mind."

"This single technique has benefited thousands of people across all walks of life – corporate executives, trauma affected, underprivileged, children and homemakers."

"I was already teaching meditation and yoga. But I felt there was something that was lacking. Though people do their spiritual practices, their life is in compartments. They do their prayers, meditation and spiritual practices, but when they come out in life, they are very different people. So, I was thinking how we can bridge this gap – between inner silence and outer expression of life.
During a period of silence, the Sudarshan Kriya came like an inspiration. After I came out of the silence, I started teaching whatever I knew and people had great experiences."

"After Sudarshan Kriya, many people feel so pure and so clear, so complete, because the consciousness, which was stuck in the matter, material, which is foreign to itself, got released from that and came back to its home. That is the sense of purity, feeling of purity."

"We need to do a cleansing process within ourselves. In sleep, we get rid of fatigue, but the deeper stresses remain in our body. Sudarshan Kriya cleanses the system from the inside. The breath has a great secret to offer."

SADHANA

"*Sadhana* – Sanskrit word for spiritual practices *Seva*–Sanskrit that means service. Happiness and freedom are within you. They have always been inside you."

"*Sadhana* happens when all the efforts are dropped. When you are totally relaxed, you experience true bliss."

"Root out boredom through deep and continued meditation."

"If you are unable to meditate because your mind is chattering too much, just feel that you are a little stupid, and then you will be able to sink deep into meditation."

"Meditation erases the impressions and improves the expression."

"Anytime you are confused, your mind is in conflict, do asanas, sit in asana. You will see, right away, clarity comes."

"Effect of asana is clearing out of all conflicts, duality."

"The seed of negativity and the tendency for conflict in you can only
be annihilated by *sadhana*."

"*Sadhana* helps you to maintain your centeredness and not be shaken by small events."

"*Sadhana* is meant to increase this prana level in you. If your *prana* level is constantly high - then you don't need to do *sadhana* - that is what is enlightenment; your optimum *prana*."

"Spiritual blossoming' means expanding in all dimensions – being happy, at ease with yourself, and with everybody around you."

SILENCE

"Prayer within breath is silence. Love within infinity is silence. Wisdom without words is silence. Compassion without aim is silence."

"Mind without agitation is meditation. Mind in the present moment is meditation. Mind that has no hesitation, no anticipation is meditation. Mind that has come back home, to the source, is meditation. Mind that becomes, 'no mind' is meditation."

"Silence is the goal of all answers. If an answer does not silence the mind, it is no answer."

"Only silence is complete."

"Smiling with all the existence is silence."

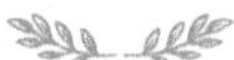

"Purpose of words is to create silence."

"Listen to others; yet do not listen. If your mind gets stuck in their problems, not only are they miserable, but you also become miserable."

SATSANG

"Why do people need homes? Can they live without shelter like animals in the forest? Man needs protection from changing elements of nature, so he builds a shelter for physical comforts. In the same way, for spiritual and mental comfort, *satsang* is the shelter."

"Question: What about the pleasure in *satsang*?
Answer: The pleasure of *satsang* takes you towards expansion."

"Give quality time to the divine, it will be rewarded. Give *satsang* and meditation your highest priority."

"One who does not do *satsang* is like a wild animal. *Satsang* alone makes you civilized."

"*Satsang* is the shelter from changing time and its harsh influence on life."

FREEDOM

"Real freedom is the freedom from the future and freedom from the past. When you are not happy in the present moment, then you desire for a bright future."

"One who has given you everything has also given you freedom. Honour the freedom and make good use of all things given to you."

"Break through the barrier of the rational mind and find freedom for yourself."

"Freedom is your very nature. Only with freedom do joy, generosity and other human values blossom."

"Just an intention to be free makes you immediately free."

"Freedom without discipline is like a country without a defence."

"If even the slightest desire to be free has arisen in you, you should pat yourself on the back, you are very lucky. Billions of lives on this planet don't have this blessing. They do not even live. They exist, die and dissolve. They are not bored. Even if they are bored, they're bored about something very small. A little change can make them very comfortable again. So, blessed are those who get bored!"

FAITH

"In spirituality, faith is first and knowledge comes later. Like Sudarshan Kriya, *pranayama*, yoga asanas and meditation – first you have faith and then knowledge follows."

"Science considers even human beings as matter; spirituality considers even earth as mother, even rivers and mountains as living beings."

"Faith and alertness appear to be completely opposite in nature. When you are alert, usually there is no faith and you feel restless and insecure. When there is faith, the mind is secure and rested and you are not alert."

"If you have complete faith, there are no questions. If you have no faith there is no point in asking any questions because how can there be any faith in the answer you receive?"

"If you lack faith, you have to pray for faith. But to pray, you need faith. This is a paradox."

"Faith in yourself brings freedom.
Faith in the world brings you peace of mind.
Faith in God evokes love in you."

"Question: What is the difference between faith and confidence?
Sri Sri: Confidence is the result. Faith is the beginning."

EGO

"Ego is always ambitious and wants to do the toughest job like climbing Mount Everest, etc. Whereas in a simple act like watching a butterfly, watering the garden, watching the birds or the sky, can bring deep relaxation."

"Ego is that something, which has two aspects – the positive and the negative. The creativity in you – are the results of ego. At the same time, when you break down communication, when you isolate yourself, when you're in tears, when you're stressed – that is also ego."

"The 'I' or ego in you is a tiny atom. If this atom is associated with the body, the matter, it identifies with the matter. If this atom is put with the Being, the Infinite, it identifies with the Infinite."

"Ego is separateness, non-belongingness."

"The head level is safe for the ego. The heart level breaks the ego. The soul level dissolves the ego."

"The inability to communicate occurs because of ego."

"Someone experiences bliss, and that bliss, itself becomes a trip for the ego. So the ego, in turn, destroys the infinity, the joy, and the bliss."

ENLIGHTENMENT

"Enlightenment is beyond seasons like the evergreen coconut tree."

"Seekers on the spiritual path are curious to know about enlightenment. What is enlightenment? I say, enlightenment is like a joke! It is like a fish in the ocean searching for the ocean."

"Buddha got enlightened under the Bodhi tree. He then stood up and watched the tree from a distance for seven days. He took sixteen steps towards the tree and under each step, blossomed a Lotus flower. This is the legend."

"The Bodhi tree is symbolic of both *Sansara* (world) and *Dharma*. The Lotus flower symbolizes clarity, dispassion, love, beauty and purity."

"It is only when you are detached in life, you can watch."

SURRENDER

"Do not say that you want to surrender. Just know that you already are surrendered."

"We think surrender is a sign of weakness, when in fact it is a sign of strength. Surrender comes with knowledge, with realisation and with gratefulness."

"A person who cannot surrender cannot be self-reliant."

"When you are shaken, remember the foundation of responsibility
is surrender."

"The greatest power is in surrender, surrender to the Divine."

WISDOM

"Drop all the divisions (of the mind), altogether. This is what is holding you back from enlightenment. This is what is holding you back from your very nature. Drop those right now."

"Your own judgement brings the barrier, separates you, and makes you behave so funnily. When you are judging, you are judging your own self, but you are super-imposing it on this, or this, or this, or this, or this."

"The entire universe is just an expression, projection, of the Being, of the Self. Within this small body, you are able to experience the infinite space."

"Though enlightenment is one in the world, there are many different flavours."

"A poor man celebrates the new year once a year. A rich man celebrates each day. But the richest man celebrates every moment."

"Abiding in the self you become the valentine for the whole world. Spirit is the valentine of matter and matter is the valentine of the spirit."

"There is no criteria for enlightenment. You have it already. When will it come out, when will it blossom, is completely a mystery."

"The world appears imperfect on the surface but underneath, all is perfect. Perfection hides, imperfection shows off."

"Sincerity is being in touch with your depth."

"You are total. You are full. You have all that you need.
Do not underestimate yourself."

"A devotee will never fall. He cannot fall. There is no chance for it."

"Abundance is a state of mind within you. If you just look at 'lack',
the lack increases in life."

"The best 'puja', the best form of worship, is to be happy, to be grateful."

"Behind every activity, pleasant, unpleasant, chaotic, harmonious, is one Divinity."

"Basing your life on words is very superficial."

"Whatever you want for others will happen to you."

"See a mistake as a mistake, not as 'my' or 'his' mistake. 'My' means guilt; 'his' means anger."

"Want is always hanging on to the 'I'. When the 'I' itself is dissolving, 'want' also dissolves, disappears."

"See ninety per cent of this body is only space. And what is in this space? That is mind; that is consciousness; that is intelligence."

"Without being critical, the intellect cannot progress. But that criticism should not come from the heart, it can come from the throat."

"If any has to be given, this is the blessing that has to be given—be devoid of feverishness."

"The Self is the centre of the whole creation."

"If you are passionate, be passionate for the highest, the most wonderful, and the most beautiful. Be passionate for this entire creation. Everything is so beautiful."

"Truth cannot be understood through proof. Anything that can be proven can be disproven also. Truth is beyond proof or disproof."

"Take a while and just relax. Repose in the depth of your being."

"Forgetfulness is one of the greatest blessings."

"Events cannot stick on to you. You are like the pure crystal. *Niranjanah*-untouched, unstained by anything."

"Beauty has three levels: indication, expression, and exposure. Spirituality indicates, art expresses, and science exposes."

"You are Divine. You are part of me. I am part of you."

"Life is a package of surprise gifts for you."

"When heart speaks and heart listens, harmony is produced. It is always so. When head talks and head listens, argument is produced."

"*Sadhyojata* means creating every moment anew, knowing every moment new. We are used to a certain dimension, so this may go beyond you."

"Difference between motivation and inspiration –motivation is external and short lived. Inspiration is internal and lifelong."

SUCCESS

"Don't think of anything as difficult. Know that we have an even greater power within and according to that we get tasks to do."

"There is nothing to worry about. There will be tough times, nice times, good times and bad times. They all come in life and go. Nothing stays."

"If you want to make sense it has to come from silence."

"Forgive yourself and forgive others. Don't chew on other's mistakes
or your own mistakes."

"Welcome each day with a genuine smile from within."

"Grace has the ability to change anything at any time."

"Don't fall in love, rise in love."

"Turn your demand into gratefulness. The more grateful you are, more love comes your way."

"Never label yourself. Learn from the past and move on. Feelings come and go. They are never stationary. Neither blame others nor yourself."

"Stress is too much to do, too little time, and no energy. It can be difficult to reduce your workload, or increase the time that you have, but you can increase your energy level."

EDUCATION

"When life has commitment towards human values such as compassion and nonviolence, then life flows in a proper direction."

"The purpose of education is to build good, strong and talented personality. Spirituality is that which builds you into a wonderful personality."

"Enlightenment is returning back to simplicity, honesty, love and faith that truth will triumph or succeed."

"Often one does not even know why one is in a hurry. It almost becomes a biological phenomenon to be in a rush. Wake up and become aware of the rush in you!"

"Neither denying nor striving helps to solve problems. Solutions happen when you are calm and collected, you use intelligence, you are not lethargic but active and you have strong faith in Divine law."

SPIRITUALITY

"Attaining a spiritual level is simply recognizing there is life everywhere, that there is spirit everywhere."

"Spirituality is a harmonious blend of outer silence and inner celebration, and also inner silence and outer celebration."

"Spirituality gives you strength, that inner strength to manage difficult situations and to keep you ever smiling."

"The source of your mind is love and whatever you do to go to that source is a spiritual practice."

"The knowledge which gives us a broad vision and a big heart is spirituality."

"To grow in unconditional love and in beauty is spirituality."

"The food of spirituality is love, joy, compassion and beauty."

"Spiritual blossoming simply means blossoming in life in all dimensions – being happy, at ease with yourself and with everybody around you."

"The moment you feel the connection from your side, just know that you are already connected, otherwise,you won't even come near this knowledge, this path."

"Spirituality is nothing but caring and sharing, offering oneself in service."

"Finding security in inner space is spirituality."

HAPPINESS

"In joy, in peace, in that soothing-very soothing-inner state, you will find happiness."

"You should be ready for any challenge. This readiness will make you happy.

"Every moment that you spend here on this planet, know that you are for a unique, big purpose, for greater than just to eat, sleep and talk. You are here for a greater cause. Just remember that. Take a challenge- 'Come what may I am going to smile today and be happy!'"

"All of one's life is spent in preparing to be happy someday in the future. It's like making your bed all night, but having no time to sleep in it."

"There are two ways of looking at life. One is thinking, 'I'll be happy after achieving a certain objective.' The second is saying, 'I am happy come what may!"

"How much time is left for giving love and smiling? Just a few years. In our entire life, this is the time that we really lived. The rest of the time is spent on preparing to live."

"Knowledge is a burden if it robs you of innocence.
Knowledge is a burden if it is not integrated into life.
Knowledge is a burden if it doesn't bring joy.
Knowledge is a burden if it gives you an idea that you are wise.
Knowledge is a burden if it doesn't set you free.
Knowledge is a burden if it makes you feel you are special."

A robust Guru mantra to eclipse ignorance